# DAPHNE TF

# Angelina Dexter

ARTHUR H. STOCKWELL LTD.
Torrs Park Ilfracombe Devon
*Established 1898*
*www.ahstockwell.co.uk*

ISBN 0 7223 3522-9
*Printed in Great Britain by*
*Arthur H. Stockwell Ltd.*
*Torrs Park   Ilfracombe*
*Devon*

# INTRODUCTION

For many years it has been my desire to put together a simple biography of the life of a fine "Lady", who I admire so much and to whom I can personally relate.

Someone who, although born in London in 1907, regularly visited Cornwall on family holidays at an early age, where she acquired the taste for the rural West Country life, particularly around the area of Fowey. Here she lived most happily until she sadly died in 1989 at the age of eighty-two.

We Cornish folk are very proud of our "adopted cousin", I mean of course Lady Browning — DAME DAPHNE du MAURIER.

I understand only too well how she felt because I too like being alone.

This is my story of this great lady.

*Angelina Dexter, 2002*

# ACKNOWLEDGEMENTS

To the du Maurier family for the hours of pleasure that they have given me during the creation of this book.

My appreciation to the publishers, Arthur H. Stockwell Ltd., of Ilfracombe, Devon, who made my dream come true.

My gratitude to the proprietors of The Jamaica Inn for allowing me to print the picture of their Cornish Inn, painted by Mr Wilf Plowman, on the front cover.

To my husband, Ivor, with thanks for reminding me to keep going when at times I had given up and left it all to gather dust.

Finally, I would like to mention my dear departed parents Edna and Joseph Dexter who made 'Joe's Maid' what she is today.

The map shows the main roads through Cornwall and areas where the general action of the Cornish novels takes place.

1. The King's General
2. Jamaica Inn
3. The King's General
4. The Loving Spirit
   Frenchman's Creek
   Castle Dor
   Rebecca
   My Cousin Rachel
   The Birds
   The House on the Strand
   Rule Britannia
5. Castle Dor
6. The House on the Strand
7. Frenchman's Creek
   Jamaica Inn

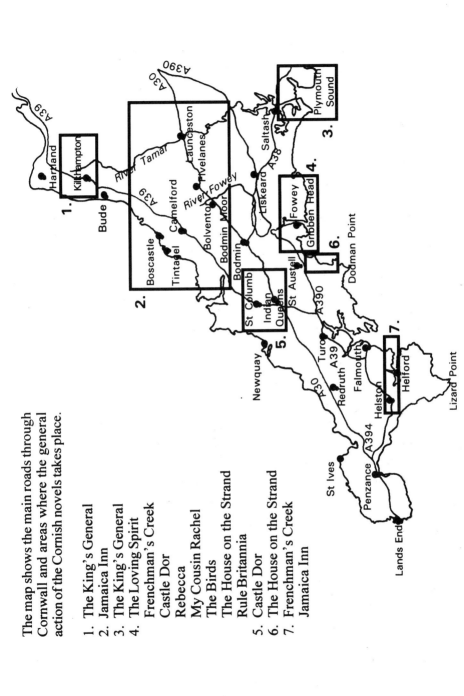

# THE WORK OF DAPHNE du MAURIER

## BOOKS — (First Publications)

| Date | Name |
|------|------|
| 1931 | The Loving Spirit. |
| 1932 | I'll Never be Young Again. |
| 1933 | The Progress of Julius. |
| 1934 | Gerald.* |
| 1936 | Jamaica Inn. |
| 1937 | The du Mauriers.* |
| 1938 | Rebecca. |
| 1940 | Come Wind. Come Weather. |
| 1941 | Frenchman's Creek. |
| 1943 | Hungry Hill. |
| 1946 | The King's General. |
| 1949 | The Parasites. |
| 1951 | My Cousin Rachel. |
| 1954 | Mary Anne.* |
| 1957 | The Scapegoat. |
| 1960 | The Infernal World of Branwell Brontë.* |
| 1962 | Castle Dor. *(Started by "Q".)* |
| 1963 | The Glass Blowers. *(Semifiction)* |
| 1965 | The Flight of the Falcon. |
| 1967 | Vanishing Cornwall.* |
| 1969 | The House On The Strand. |
| 1972 | Rule Britannia. |
| 1975 | Golden Lads.* |
| 1976 | The Winding Stair.* |
| 1977 | Growing Pains.* |
| 1981 | The Rebecca Notebooks. |

1975 Golden Lads.* } *(About the Bacon Bros. —*
1976 The Winding Stair.* } *Antony and Francis Bacon)*

\* *Nonfiction*

## FILM ADAPTATIONS

1.  Jamaica Inn.
2.  Rebecca.
3.  Frenchman's Creek.
4.  Hungry Hill.
5.  My Cousin Rachel.
6.  The Scapegoat.
7.  The Birds. ⎱
8.  Don't Look Now. ⎰ *From Short Story Books*


## SHORT STORIES.

| | |
|---|---|
| 1952 | The Apple Tree. |
| 1959 | The Breaking Point. |
| 1971 | Not After Midnight. |
| 1976 | Echoes From the Macabre. |
| 1980 | The Rendezvous. |


## PLAYS STAGED IN LONDON THEATRES

| | |
|---|---|
| 1939 | Rebecca. |
| 1945 | The Years Between. |
| 1949 | September Tide. |

# CONTENTS

# Chapter 1

## *Grandfather, George du Maurier*

George Louis Palmella Busson du Maurier was the eldest of three children, born in Paris in 1834 and nicknamed Kicky all his life.

He started with nothing and spent his youth travelling between London, Paris, Belgium and Boulogne, eventually arriving in England from Paris with just a few pounds in his pocket, as a young penniless artist.

In London his father wanted him to become a scientist but George himself wanted to become an opera singer which his father objected to. Instead he was placed in a laboratory, but he spent more time drawing than experimenting!

In 1856 George's father died, after which twenty-two-year-old George, with his mother, returned to Paris to study Art. A year later he went to the Antwerp Academy where, whilst drawing from a model, he suddenly lost the sight of his left eye and spent the next two years believing he was at risk of losing the sight of his other eye as well.

Consulting a German specialist he was reassured that he would not go blind, so he decided to return to London to further his career in journalism and magazine illustration, and at the age of thirty he joined the staff of *Punch* magazine — a weekly paper which quickly became a success.

Several years later, in 1863, George married Emma Wightwick and between them had five children:— Trixie (Beatrix), Guy, Sylvia, May (Marie-Louise) and Gerald, but sadly not one of them lived to old age.

During his life George became a rich man and was always well off in that late Victorian era, writing three novels; the first being: — *Peter Ibbetson*, published in 1891 which proved a very popular book at that time.

In the years to come George du Maurier was to be a great influence on his young granddaughter Daphne as a future writer herself.

Over the years the young Daphne had a crush on the famous actor Basil Rathbone, who also played the part of the wicked Lord Rockingham in Daphne's future book, *Frenchman's Creek*.

In 1894, at the age of sixty, George wrote his second novel called *Trilby* which led to a hit play, a series of films, and the trilby hat!

Throughout their married life Emma remained the devoted wife and mother, until George sadly died in 1896 at the age of sixty-two. His ashes were buried at Hampstead Church, London, followed by Emma's in 1914.

## Chapter 2

## *Father, Gerald du Maurier*

George and Emma's youngest child Gerald, born 26th March 1873, went on to become a leading actor/stage manager, and also starred in films.

On the 11th April 1903, at the age of thirty, Gerald married an actress called Muriel Beaumont, a solicitor's daughter, whom he met a year earlier when acting together in the same play, *The Admirable Crichton* at the Duke of York Theatre.

Together they had three daughters:— Angela, born 1.3.04, Daphne, born 13.5.07 and Jeanne, born 1911. All three du Maurier girls had good looks, particularly Daphne's eyes, which were lavender not blue.

Gerald, Muriel and their three girls were a happy family. He the breadwinner of the family, Muriel the devoted wife and mother, the complete homemaker, giving up her own acting career to care for her growing family; belonging to an age of plenty and gracious living.

Gerald became one of the most successful actors of his day, at thirty-three playing *Raffles*, the suave cricketer jewel thief turned cracksman, his first big acting success at the Wyndham Theatre, Charing Cross Road. He spent the next fifteen years there in various productions, and, through the theatre, became a friend of Edgar Wallace.

Gerald was always attracted to women — as they were to him — but he always remained with his wife and daughters even though he had numerous affairs — the last one with Gracie Fields.

By now Gerald was being well paid, moving house and family to Regents Park with nannies, servants, nurse, parlour maids and a cook. Hence, a busy life for Gerald and Muriel.

Both Angela and Jeanne never married, but so this fascinating family story continues with the life of the young Daphne du Maurier.

## Chapter 3

## *Daphne du Maurier*

Born in 1907, Daphne as a child was used to living in a large house called Cannon Hall, with private education at home by a governess called Miss Waddell, Tod for short, who was eventually lured away by an offer from Constantinople to teach English to the daughters of the then sultan.

Governess Dora Vigo took her place and continued to teach Daphne and Jeanne, whilst young Angela had gone off to a Paris finishing school and was now on her own two feet with an allowance from her father.

Governess Tod eventually returned from Constantinople and frequently visited the du Maurier family at their house, Cannon Hall, and soon Daphne herself went on to a Paris finishing school. Throughout her youth she always enjoyed writing, and lived in a continual dream world.

Around this time the wireless had arrived! Angela had her voice trained, Jeanne did well playing the piano, drawing and painting, but Daphne could only write!

# Chapter 4

## *The First World War*

By the outbreak of the First World War in 1914, Gerald and the actress Gladys Cooper, experienced a most successful stage relationship, followed by a grim year; Gerald's mother Emma died in 1914 at the age of seventy-one, to be buried with her husband George, followed by the death of his brother Guy, who was killed in France in 1915.

The following year of 1916, Gerald moved his family to Hampstead to continue a very privileged lifestyle.

Although the three girls were used to visiting their father in the theatre, Daphne never enjoyed the theatrical social life of the du Maurier family, preferring to be on her own.

With the ending of the war in 1918, Gerald decided, at forty-five years of age, to join up as a soldier with the Irish Guards but this proved to be a short stay only. In the years which followed he returned to the theatre in a play called *Bulldog Drummond*, but it was proving not so easy to make money now as an actor.

# Chapter 5

## *The Postwar Years*

In 1922 Gerald was knighted and fifteen-year-old Daphne began writing short stories and spent the next year enjoying summer holidays and Christmas in Monte Carlo and Cannes.

The family governess/teacher, Dora Vigo, was soon to marry and become Mrs Mead, but continued teaching until the autumn of 1924, when she departed expecting a baby the following March.

In 1924 Angela, back home in England, was cast as Wendy in *Peter Pan* and was visited in her dressing room afterwards by the famous actress Tallulah Bankhead, whilst Daphne, at the age of seventeen, was sent away to the Paris finishing school, after spending many years of special tuition at home with the family governess.

Here she met Mlle Yvon Fernande, a French teacher about thirty years of age, who never married due to the fact that her fiancé Marcel was killed in the 1914-18 War which left her heartbroken. Daphne was devoted to her, to the extent of an intense crush on her which lasted for many years, resulting in them becoming very close, intimate friends. Much later it was said it was nothing more than a mother/daughter relationship, right up until Yvon's own early death

17

from leukaemia in middle-age.

By now Daphne had obtained a typewriter and was well into serious writing, but at this time she developed a spot on her lungs and was losing a lot of weight.

Then came 1926 and the General Strike, with no tubes, no trains and no buses. Gerald was acting and producing *The Ringer* by Edgar Wallace at the Wyndham Theatre, which proved a great success.

Daphne was now nineteen years of age, continuing to write her short stories and at the same time, although given a generous allowance by her father, had this strong desire to be independent, and spent a lot of holiday time in France and Switzerland with her French friend Fernande, who was not well due to exhaustion and heart trouble.

Her sister Angela was happy to live at home, whilst Jeanne attended a day school in Hampstead, both girls having plenty of friends. Daphne didn't want any, and was happy to join the Hampstead Library — the subscription being paid by her mother.

# Chapter 6

## *Ferryside*

In 1926 Gerald decided to buy a big family country house for holidays, by the sea in Cornwall. So in September 1926, Muriel and her three daughters went down to Looe in Cornwall to look for this holiday house.

This area proved unsuccessful, so they moved on to the nearby Fowey estuary, strolling around Polruan and the Bodinnick Ferry area.

On the way to The Ferry Inn for lunch that day, they saw a For Sale notice on the gate of the old rambling boat yard, with a flat called Swiss Cottage, right alongside the Bodinnick Ferry. So Gerald bought it, and the long love affair with this house began for the du Maurier family which continues today. It was soon to be renamed Ferryside because the family didn't like the original name as it reminded them of the underground railway in London!

Here, was the freedom that Daphne was looking for to peacefully write, walk, boat, and be alone!

The original boathouse comprised three stories:— 1. a ground floor to build boats; 2. sail lofts; 3. top floor — living accommodation. The back wall of the house was the actual rock of the cliff behind, and the house was painted white.

All through the winter of 1926 and the spring of 1927, Muriel set forth to modernise the new holiday home, employing tradesmen such as builders and decorators, to gut the old boat house and make Ferryside habitable for the family to live in, when they were away from their London home.

Buying Ferryside changed Daphne's life forever. Cornwall became so important to her — more than London or even France. She soon decided to study on her own in the Cornish peaceful atmosphere, writing a play, poetry and more short stories.

During the spring of 1927, whilst all the building work progressed at Ferryside, Daphne went off to Paris to meet her friend Fernande. Then on to Switzerland where Edgar Wallace had invited her and her sister Angela, to join his party of family and friends to skate and ski — a winter sports holiday. From there she went to Berlin for a week with her father, who by now was aware that his daughter was something of a loner.

By May 1927, when Daphne was just twenty years of age, the holiday home by the River Fowey was transformed and ready for occupation. The 1st floor of the old storeroom, where boats were built in the old days, was now the living room with a staircase leading to the floor above. This 2nd floor, instead of sail lofts, were now bedrooms and a bathroom, and the top floor became Gerald and Muriel's area, together with a bathroom, dining room and kitchen.

Muriel and Angela went down to Fowey to order the carpets, curtains and furniture, finding it no longer an old ferry house, but altered into a luxury holiday home for the du Maurier family and their three/four Pekingese dogs.

Once their house was in order Muriel and Angela returned to London, but Daphne stayed behind to explore the Cornish countryside on her own, preferring gardening and walking to housework, and was never bored or depressed in this rural environment compared to her home in London.

She soon met for the first time the neighbours who lived on the opposite side of the river in a house called The Haven, belonging to Sir Arthur Quiller-Couch, known as "Q", who was knighted in 1910 — and so began a long friendship.

## Chapter 7

# *Jane Slade*

Enjoying their first summer of 1927 at their new riverside house, Gerald soon had a motor cruiser built named *Cora Ann,* (after the heroine in Edgar Wallace's *The Ringer*), for family outings on the River Fowey, but Daphne, liking her own independence, wanted her own sailing boat.

Continuing to write daily until 1 p.m., then walking in the local woods in the afternoon, she came upon Pont Creek with the tide out and full of old relics. This creek, an estuary of the Fowey river between Bodinnick and Polruan, contained one relic which particularly interested Daphne. It was the old *Jane Slade*, a derelict, rotting, abandoned schooner, but strangely enough, her figurehead of a young woman was still intact. This old wreck haunted Daphne and was the inspiration of her first novel, *The Loving Spirit*.

It seems a Jane Slade had been the mother of the man who built this old schooner, down at the boat yard at nearby Polruan. When the hulk was broken up Daphne was given this figurehead which she had placed on the corner of Ferryside outside her bedroom window overlooking the Fowey harbour, where she spent so much of her time writing.

The original Jane Slade was buried at the local Lanteglos-by-Fowey church where Daphne herself was to marry her future soldier husband in 1932.

# Chapter 8

## *Life in Fowey*

During this Cornish summer of 1927 Gerald became bored in Fowey, especially in poor weather, and therefore invited visitors to call at his home for company, much to Daphne's dislike. She by now was dressing in the local habit of a seaman's life, in her much-loved sea boots, sweaters and sou'westers.

Continuing her happy life with her sister Angela, spending her time walking, writing and using her father's boat, the *Cora Ann*, she remarked that Fowey meant more to her now than anything else. She enjoyed the river harbour and the sea so very much, compared to "dreary London".

In the autumn Daphne spent a month in Paris with her friend Fernande, returning in time to spend Christmas at the beloved Ferryside in Cornwall.

New Year 1928 was spent getting to know the friendly villagers by name and visiting The Haven for Sunday tea with "Q", who at that time suggested she had a sailing boat of her own built.

In the April it was Gerald and Muriel's Silver Wedding Anniversary, with a family celebration lunch held at The Savoy in London.

On Daphne's twenty-first birthday, 13th May 1928, her mother presented her with a rowing boat which was named *Annabelle Lee,* to go with the sailing boat Daphne was having built locally and to be named the *Marie-Louise* (after her Aunt May).

It was being built at the Polruan boat yard by the Slade Brothers; the well-seasoned wood from the nearby Lerryn woods being used for its keel. Daphne watched its construction with great interest. It was to be ready by September for its maiden voyage, but due to the autumn gales, it was soon laid-up until the following spring.

Ferryside became Daphne's base, where she continued her writing to help pay for its upkeep, but still spent time walking the lovely Cornish countryside.

## Chapter 9

## *Exploring Menabilly*

It was on one of these walks one day, via the Gribben Head that
Daphne and Angela noticed a grey roof peeping through the trees
across the river which aroused great interest. On making some
enquiries she was informed that the bit of the old house they could
see was called Menabilly — owned by a Dr Rashleigh, a magistrate
in Devon who rarely lived there. (The Rashleigh's being an old
West Country family dating as far back as the 13th Century.)

So intrigued by this house of history, Daphne asked "Q" for more
details, and was duly told he used to visit Menabilly in its heyday for
garden parties, but that the present owner disliked it, due to unhappy
memories of the old house in his youth.

Very anxious to see more of Menabilly, Daphne, Angela and her
dog, set off again one afternoon to find the interesting house that
she could only see the roof top of, and eventually came upon a
derelict, overgrown driveway which twisted and turned for about
three miles.

As the winter light was fading they decided to come back again
the next day to explore further, and this time they found another
driveway to the house which Angela thought frightening, lonely and

gloomy — truly a house of secrets which Daphne would grow to love.

Reaching the old house, they looked through some windows to see a sad sight of dusty furniture, but to Daphne it was love at first sight! In spite of all the neglect and gloomy-covered ivy outside, she was determined to live there one day!

In April 1929, Daphne rose early at 5 a.m. to row her boat to Pridmouth Cove, below Menabilly, to once again trespass and prowl around the old house which constantly haunted her. Eventually she reached the lawn, and there before her stood Menabilly!

# Chapter 10

## *The Loving Spirit*

Around this time Gerald's theatrical career and his extravagant lifestyle became more difficult to finance, so Daphne was soon to take two major steps in her life — to write her first novel, *The Loving Spirit* (later to be published in 1931), and, within two years, to marry her soldier husband, Tommy Browning.

By September 1929 Ferryside was empty of visitors and shut up for the winter to economise. Daphne lodged with a Miss Roberts at The Nook cottage opposite Ferryside where there was no bathroom, only a hipbath and a toilet up the garden path.

At Ferryside, at twenty-two years of age, she started her first novel, taken from a line in a poem by Emily Brontë, continuing to write in the morning and rowing and walking in the afternoon.

Part one was finished in two weeks and part two by the 17th November 1929.

## Chapter 11

## *Life Continues*

Now that the Cornish winter was upon her and feeling a little bored, Daphne went off for Christmas to Switzerland with the family friends of Edgar Wallace, and met the young actor and future film director Carol Reed. Both of whom were twenty-two at the time and went on to become very good friends; he writing daily letters from London to Daphne down in Cornwall. At the time he had a small part in the Edgar Wallace play a *The Calendar*, performing at the Wyndham Theatre where he stage-managed as well.

Daphne deeply loved her father Gerald but disliked his theatrical social life, preferring the rural life down in the West Country (until Ferryside became alive with visitors once more).

A strong emotional bond developed between Gerald and his daughters, although Daphne indicated she was never a sexy person, but marrying her future husband meant a great deal to her. She only realised how much after his death, when the marital physical side of life proved not to be important to her any longer.

Life carried on in Cornwall as usual, writing, walking, sailing, rabbiting, fishing and tea on Sundays at The Haven with "Q", the son of a Cornish doctor, who called Fowey in his own books, Troy Town. His daughter Foy, named after Fowey, he was also a JP and so began a very long friendship with young Daphne.

## Chapter 12

## *A Privileged Lifestyle*

With hard times in the theatre, due to the depression, Gerald's financial situation was pursued by the Inland Revenue. To help out this situation, Gerald *lent* his family name to a new cigarette to be named Du Maurier Cigarettes purely for the financial reward.

At this time his health also began to decline, due to a persistent cough. The financial worries also brought on depression due to the fact that he was unable to accept growing old.

Daphne was now living a highly privileged lifestyle; travelling to London to see Carol Reed — back to Fowey — sailing her *Marie-Louise* — visiting "Q" and his daughter Foy for tea — over to Paris to visit her friend Fernande plus holiday parties to Europe.

During the winter of 1929/30, and back living in Fowey with Miss Roberts at The Nook, Daphne tackled part four of her first novel, *The Loving Spirit*, for which "Q" found her a typist (a Mrs Smith) to type parts one to three of her completed manuscripts.

By the end of January 1930 the final part of this book was completed and sent to Mrs Smith for typing — all originally handwritten by Daphne — approx. 200,000 words in three months. Afterwards she went off to Paris to stay once again with Fernande.

## Chapter 13

## *The Summer of 1930*

After this holiday Daphne's second novel was in her mind, and by the end of March 1930 she commenced *I'll Never Be Young Again*, which was finished four months later.

May arrived and the twenty-third birthday of Daphne. Her friend Carol Reed was in London acting in a play at The Shaftsbury Theatre, whilst she herself was getting no peace for her writing down at Ferryside, due to the arrival of family and friends for summer visitations to the riverside house. It became so hectic with noisy laughter and chat, that it drove Daphne out of the house to once again explore Menabilly.

At first Daphne became a trespasser in and around this nearby estate, and would walk all around the big house, covered in creeping ivy and dust, which still haunted her by its obvious past.

There were two great families of Fowey — the Rashleighs and the Treffrys, and "Q" suggested she should write to Dr Rashleigh, the present owner of Menabilly, to ask for permission to walk around his grounds. She was duly introduced to Alice Rashleigh who had lived there as a young girl.

Dr Rashleigh replied and agreed, so Daphne spent the summer

of 1930 lovingly exploring it, but at the same time, visiting parts of Cornwall with her friend, Foy Quiller-Couch. She met other well-known Cornish families, such as: Cecilie Rogers, Lady Vyvyan at Trelowarren, a 16th Century stonehouse on The Lizard where, on the south side of this estate, was Frenchman's Pill (Frenchman's Creek) on the Helford river. (Lady Vyvyan eventually left Frenchman's Pill and the land to the National Trust.)

By the end of September 1930 Ferryside was at last free of visitors, and to economise once again Muriel shut up their riverside house — Daphne again staying nearby with Miss Roberts, who catered for her every need.

Two months later Daphne was off with Foy, in mild weather, up to Bodmin Moor on two horses, to stay at the Jamaica Inn hostelry, an old coaching stop of bygone days, halfway between Bodmin and Launceston in the hamlet of Bolventor. On the way home bad weather set in across the moors, but the two horses brought their two riders back to Fowey by pure instinct.

Christmas 1930 was spent with the du Maurier family in London, together with Carol Reed, followed by a trip over to Paris to see Fernande.

On her return Daphne commenced her third novel, *The Progress of Julius* at Ferryside, as well as gardening, sailing, and her usual visits to "Q".

During April/May 1931, when Carol Reed was in America for three months, Daphne and Foy went on another horseriding expedition, this time to the Helford river, by way of a pony and jingle.

## Chapter 14

## *Daphne's Destiny*

It is now the summer of 1931, and at this point in her life Daphne was to meet her destiny — Frederick Arthur Montague Browning — Tommy (or Boy to his Army friends). He was a thirty-five-year-old Suffolk fellow, almost six feet tall, attractive and extrovert from an Army family. Ex-Eton/Sandhurst, he became a major in the Grenadier Guards and served in the 1914-18 War with distinction. He was awarded the DSO and the French *Croix de Guerre* at only twenty years of age — hence the nickname of Boy! He was an athletic outdoor type who represented England in the high hurdles at one of the Olympic Games. When first meeting Daphne he was a regimental officer — a major in the guards with a pilot's licence.

By September 1931 Tommy Browning and a friend sailed into Fowey harbour in Browning's white cabin cruiser, named *Ygdrasil* (taken from Norse mythology, meaning Tree of Fate), but called Yggy for short. Drawn to Cornwall having just read Daphne's newly-published first novel, *The Loving Spirit*, he enjoyed it so much he wanted to meet the author!

It was her sister Angela who first noticed him in her field glasses from Ferryside, and told Daphne about this most attractive man

c

who had been going up and down the River Fowey for weeks in a white motorboat. But Daphne wanted to finish her book *The Progress of Julius*, and at that time wasn't feeling too well herself because of appendicitis.

Two months later her third novel was finished, having taken her nine months to write, and from her publishers, Heinemann of London, Daphne received her largest cheque to date — £67 — an advance payment for *The Loving Spirit*.

Christmas 1931 was spent in Hampstead with a large family gathering which included her friend Carol Reed, who was back home again from America.

By New Year 1932 having done too much at Ferryside that autumn — felling trees, sawing wood, etc., Daphne experienced more pain and nausea due to the flare-up of her appendix, and by April 1932 was taken into hospital for its removal, returning to Fowey afterwards to recuperate.

Tommy returned to the area again, and hearing of her recent operation sent her a note saying "Sorry to hear you have been unwell, etc., and couldn't sail your boat for a while. Would you like to join me on the river in mine?" He also added that both their fathers had been members of the London Garrick Club.

Feeling flattered, Daphne replied "I would be delighted" and was soon to join Tommy on board his boat, finding him terrific fun and easy going, and afterwards spending the evening at Ferryside talking for hours over a roaring fire.

Being thirty-five years old and single, Tommy Browning had had plenty of experience in the company of women. They spent the next two days together, before he rejoined his battalion, promising to return as soon as possible.

One week later, he found her in the garden at Ferryside sawing up logs for the fire — he having driven down from London through the night to Cornwall. Daphne was hooked!

## Chapter 15

## *The Summer Wedding of 1932*

Daphne's second book *I'll Never Be Young Again* was published in May 1932, by which time Daphne was on her way to be financially independent.

Their courtship was a short one, Daphne confessing, "He was good." So Tommy spent the next couple of months in Fowey, going everywhere together, walking, river trips and being introduced to all her friends. (The naming of his boat The Tree of Fate proved very appropriate!)

By the end of June 1932 the happy couple became engaged and decided to marry. They had to inform Tommy's mother and Daphne's parents, and of course break the news to her friend Carol Reed by letter.

And so by the first week of July 1932 the couple visited her parents in London, where it was decided that they would have to live near Tommy's battalion when married, so Gerald and Muriel offered them a cottage at Cannon Hall.

On the 8th July 1932 their engagement was officially announced. Daphne hated all the fuss. She just wanted to marry and then disappear to live her quiet life.

The Press Announcement in the *Daily Telegraph* read — "Miss du Maurier's Romance, to wed Guardsman." Daphne was twenty-five, Tommy was thirty-five.

Both not wanting anything big, they were married at Lanteglos-by-Fowey church in Cornwall, on the 19th July 1932 at 8.15 a.m., because of the tide times, as the wedding party arrived at the church in two boats — The *Cora Ann,* with Gerald, Muriel, Daphne, and Geoffrey, her cousin, as best man, and the *Ygdrasil*, with Tommy and the Hunkin family as witnesses. (Both Angela and Jeanne were away at the time, so were unable to attend.)

After the short ceremony the wedding party returned to the two boats and sailed back to Ferryside where Daphne wanted no fuss — no reception — no speeches — all very simple and quiet for Mrs Browning.

The happy couple then embarked on Tommy's boat, which was quickly loaded with stores, and off they sailed down the River Fowey and out to sea, down the English Channel en route to Frenchman's Creek on the Helford river for their honeymoon.

The next day a brief note of their wedding was announced in *The Times*, re: Major F. A. M. Browning and Miss D. du Maurier.

Tommy had swept Daphne off her feet so quickly that married life became a difficult job for both of them, as they had both been used to an independent lifestyle. Now, they had both lost their freedom and within a few weeks Daphne was pregnant!

# Chapter 16

## *The Arrival of Tessa*

Gerald had now returned to making films once again in order to make some money. Fortunately this proved to be a well-paid job, as he was still paying back taxes to the Inland Revenue.

Sadly his theatre friend Edgar Wallace had died of diabetes and pneumonia, so Gerald decided to return to the stage, though still suffering with his cough.

By the spring of 1933 *The Progress of Julius* was published, and in July Daphne's first daughter was born and named Tessa, after the tragic heroine in the novel *The Constant Nymph*. She was christened at Lanteglos-by-Fowey church, where Daphne and Tommy had married a year earlier.

# Chapter 17

## *Father Gerald Departs*

Gerald's health was deteriorating rapidly, and therefore made his Will on his sixty-first birthday on the 26th March 1934 — leaving everything to his wife Muriel.

After visiting many specialists his only hope was surgery, due to bowel cancer, but tragically on the 11th April 1934, the thirty-first anniversary of his wedding to Muriel, Gerald du Maurier died. Both *The Times* and the *The Daily Telegraph* reported his funeral which was strictly private. Only close relatives were present in Hampstead, after which his ashes were buried in the du Maurier grave with his mother Emma and father George (later to be joined by his wife, Muriel).

The family house of Cannon Hall was duly sold — an end to an era.

# Chapter 18

## *Jamacia Inn*

Daphne's biography of her father *Gerald* was published by the autumn of 1934. By engaging a nanny for baby Tessa she was then free to continue her writing once again, but due to Tommy's career they were constantly on the move — five times in six years, with Tommy being a stickler for routine!!

Being recently widowed Muriel decided to live with Angela and Jeanne. Daphne hated the social life in Tommy's Army career, of dinner and cocktail parties, balls, etc. Holidays in her beloved Cornwall were now very few, depending on Army leave.

At this time Daphne commenced writing her next novel *Jamaica Inn*, a temperance house, which eventually was made into a film with Charles Laughton and directed by a young Alfred Hitchcock, who Daphne did not like.

According to bookshops, this particular book of hers was the most frequently-requested novel by visitors from all over the world.

# Chapter 19

## *Flavia*

Tommy was again posted overseas for Army duties — moving again, though her writing continued. In 1936 he was posted to Egypt as commanding officer of the Grenadier Guards, together with Daphne, young Tessa and the nanny, to live in Alexandria in a large house near the beach, where there were more dinners and parties!

During that first year Daphne became pregnant again, but returned home to England in early 1937 with young Tessa at three and a half years of age, to await the birth of her second child Flavia, who arrived on the 2nd April 1937, and so named after the princess in *The Prisoner of Zenda*.

Soon afterwards Daphne returned to Egypt and Tommy, leaving Tessa and baby Flavia in England with the nanny and the two grandmothers, but being homesick Cornwall became an obsession to Daphne, so eventually they returned to England, to another house and the start of *Rebecca*.

# Chapter 20

## *Rebecca*

Tommy was now stationed at Aldershot where he rented a Tudor house called Greyfriars, near Fleet, for his growing family.

Continuing to write *Rebecca*, which took four months to complete, Daphne made no secret of the fact that she disliked all the parties and any kind of social round. For her, the duller, the better!

This latest book was a huge money-spinner and kept Tommy in boats! It was also produced for the stage and then into a film. Daphne wanted John Gielgud as Maxim de Winter in the stage version, but had to settle for Owen Nares instead. Celia Johnson played the nameless girl with Margaret Rutherford as Mrs Danvers the housekeeper.

## Chapter 21

## *The Second World War*

In 1940 *Rebecca* went on to be made into a film with Lawrence Olivier, Joan Fontaine, Judith Anderson, and George Sanders, who Daphne liked very much.

During the early war years of 1939/40 Daphne still visited Menabilly, wandering about the grounds and dreaming about it.

Whilst in Hythe she received a letter from her sister Angela, saying there was a sale of the entire contents of Menabilly, and did she want anything?

After enquiring about buying this old house, Daphne was told it was an impossibility as the house would always remain in the Rashleigh family, to be handed down to the male heirs.

Tommy moved house again to Hertfordshire, whilst Daphne settled down to write *Come Wind. Come Weather*.

With Angela and Jeanne working together much of the time — Jeanne running a market garden on a smallholding at Bodinnick with Angela as her undergardener — both became Land Army girls and Angela indulging in some writing herself.

Following Dunkirk the young Tessa and Flavia were sent away safely down to Cornwall, whilst Tommy awaited his Army orders to go abroad on war duties.

## Chapter 22

## *Kits*

1940 and a new baby was due on Armistice Day — this time they hoped for a boy.

On the 3rd November 1940 Christian Frederick du Maurier Browning was born in Hertfordshire — everyone was thrilled. He was called Kits by all and was a much-loved and wanted son.

The two girls adored him, and Daphne herself worshipped him.

## Chapter 23

## *Frenchman's Creek*

Daphne started *Frenchman's Creek* at the time when the West Country experienced the Plymouth Blitz. Her mother Muriel was not well. The Navy had taken over Ferryside at Fowey during the war, as well as The Rock Hotel in Fowey, to be used as an officers' mess by the American officers stationed in that area at that time.

Muriel, Angela and Jeanne therefore rented a house in The Esplanade at Fowey, whilst nearby, in Plymouth, a cinema was showing the film of *Jamaica Inn*.

Daphne's latest book, *Frenchman's Creek* was now completed but it was not as successful as *Rebecca*. Nevertheless it was made into a film staring Joan Fontaine (again) as Lady Dona St. Columb, and the Mexican actor Arturo de Cordova as the Pirate, together with Basil Rathbone as the wicked Lord Rockingham. Daphne disliked this film because the Californian coast was used instead of the Helford river when shooting this film. Tommy loved the book and the film, plus the music used in the film — Clair de Lune.

# Chapter 24

## *To Cornwall*

1942 and Daphne's new book *Hungry Hill*, an Irish story, was under way, whilst Plymouth was burning again.

1943 and changes! Tommy was sent to Tunisia, working under Field Marshal Montgomery, whilst Daphne (not having visited Menabilly since the early war years), took her three young children down to Cornwall, where the Navy had moved out of Ferryside and Angela and Jeanne were back in again.

Happily back in her beloved Cornwall, Daphne visited Menabilly again, and was met by a very sad sight! The springtime weather of 1943 was bad, due to severe gales. The nearby ferry was unable to run and snow fell up until May time! The shutters at Menabilly were hanging loose, windows were broken and wallpaper was hanging off the damp walls. It was easy to climb in the front windows with dust, cobwebs and mould everywhere.

Daphne immediately telephoned her solicitor to contact the owners of Menabilly in order to rent the old house from the Rashleigh family.

A week later it was confirmed that she could have a twenty-five-year lease on it, from 1943 to 1968 — it was also made quite clear it would *never* be sold to her or anyone else.

# Chapter 25

## *The Renovation of Menabilly*

At that time Daphne could easily have afforded to purchase any other house of her choice in Cornwall, but wanting Menabilly so very much, she settled on its twenty-five-year lease instead.

Menabilly was a two-storied mansion house, only three miles and a river away from Ferryside, with blood red rhododendrons encircling the lawn in front of the house. The 19th Century owners had taken away the small painted windows and replaced them with plate glass ones instead.

It was first built in the reign of Queen Elizabeth I, but in 1890 an ugly wing was attached which did not conform with the rest of the house. Because it wasn't really lived in, it eventually fell into decay and dry rot, so that part of the house became out of bounds to her growing children when living there. (In 1980, that Victorian addition was demolished because it was considered unsafe.)

This derelict old house was sleeping for years, but it took Daphne to wake it and make it habitable once again.

When Daphne saw Menabilly in 1943 the lawn was waist high to Tessa and Flavia, and the front of the house was completely covered in some sort of climbing ivy, to the extent that not even the windows were visible.

The old house, belonging to the Rashleigh family since the 17th Century, was entailed, so therefore could never be sold but only passed down to a male heir.

Apparently Dr Rashleigh's second wife didn't like it, so it was simply left unlived-in for twenty years. This large house had two vaults which were used as the Rashleigh strongrooms for storing valuables, but during the 1939/45 War, Daphne made them into air-raid shelters, where there was no electricity, only the use of candles, torches, and paraffin lamps in the event of a wartime emergency. Fortunately it was seldom used.

Now at thirty-six years of age, she signed the lease, and so began the huge task of removing the years of neglect which almost ruined it.

By now Mrs Browning was a wealthy lady, taking over this rented house which lacked electricity, water, and heating, and with a roof requiring some attention, and due to the war she experienced difficulties in employing staff to work there. Under Daphne's employment in came the architect, builders, plumbers and electricians to commence the much-needed improvements before the Browning family could possibly live there.

First, the climbing ivy was completely stripped from the front of the house. The roof and windows were repaired, whilst indoors, the carpenters were repairing the wooden floors and doors. The electrician set forth and discovered a well in the kitchen. The chimneys were swept, fires were lit and staff were employed to scrub, brush and mop-up.

The work continued throughout the summer and autumn of 1943, and during this time Daphne was asked to give a secret party at Menabilly for the American war correspondents hiding out in Fowey — sixty American journalists!

## Chapter 26

## *Christmas*

Christmas 1943 and Tommy came home to Cornwall not knowing what to expect, but found Menabilly completely habitable. The furniture vans containing stored household goods had arrived in early December. The Christmas decorations, tree and holly were all around the house, complete with hot water and a newly-installed telephone.

Daphne's long love affair with Menabilly had at last come true, but she always lived with the fear that her much-loved house and home would never belong to her, and that one day the Rashleigh family may want it back again. (Sadly, in the summer of 1969 she very reluctantly had to leave Menabilly, but her love affair with this house continued until the day she died in 1989.)

# Chapter 27

## *In Residence*

Daphne's success with the filming of her novels, *Jamaica Inn*, *Rebecca*, *Frenchman's Creek* and now *Hungry Hill*, the Irish novel starring Margaret Lockwood, resulted in great wealth for her, but she remained reclusive to the public.

She had the financial means to employ the necessary staff for Menabilly so that she could continue her writing. Staff, such as Violet and Joyce, two sisters who shared a bedroom there to undertake the domestic duties and also to help Nanny; the gardener/handyman, Mr Charles Burt and his son John, and of course the faithful governess Tod to supervise Daphne's children who were now ten, six and three years old.

Tommy's Army pay could never pay the upkeep on Menabilly or their lifestyle there, but as her writing was now paying well, and with a large estate attached to Menabilly, this was her Paradise. She seemed to have everything now, including her much-wanted son, but it was from this time that Daphne and Tommy spent much time apart, only getting together at weekends and holidays. Tommy was still attracted to women but both remained proud of each other all their lives. He of her books, she of his Army profession. The sex

49

D

side of her marriage had diminished in its importance, but their fondness and affection remained always, with Tommy finding physical fulfilment elsewhere.

Daphne still disliked any social life or public gatherings and wanted no limelight whatsoever. Tommy on the other hand was opposite due to his very full Army life, but Daphne did go to Balmoral once with him in 1954.

# Chapter 28

## *Separate Lives*

After their first Christmas together at Menabilly Tommy was promoted to lieutenant general at the young age of forty-seven. Daphne started her first book at Menabilly called *The King's General* which involved much research — a fiction book but based on fact which took up three years of her writing life.

The invasion of Normandy was forthcoming, and sadly her dear friend Sir Arthur Quiller-Couch died.

It was now 13th May 1944, Daphne's thirty-seventh birthday, and she had only seen her husband once since Christmas.

D-day — 6th June 1944. Daphne's fame and publicity now brought the photographers to Menabilly, which was not to her liking at all, as she was living a very sheltered life at the old house and only seeing a few people. She thrived on this isolation of being on her own, but was not lonely.

It was even known that some of the American GI fans, stationed in Cornwall at that time, would arrive at Menabilly in their jeeps for Daphne to sign their newly-purchased du Maurier books!

8th September 1944 — the Battle of Arnhem, on which the film *A Bridge Too Far* was based.

After the war, Daphne's two girls were sent to a boarding school, St Mary's, Wantage, in Berkshire, and in 1949 son Kits also went to a boys' boarding school, then when old enough to Eton like his father.

# Chapter 29

## *The End of the War*

During her youth Daphne had learned to drive a car, but had never kept it up, preferring to hire a taxi whenever necessary instead of owning a car. She had few outings apart from going over to Ferryside, three miles away, or for birthday treats when she would take her children to The Red Lion Hotel in Truro for lunch — a twenty mile trip each way by taxi!

One of her plays, *The Years Between*, was published in 1945, followed by *The King's General* in 1946.

Staff difficulties were being experienced at Menabilly. Nanny leaving due to ill health to stay with a friend, but being rewarded with a substantial sum of money by Daphne. She returned at a later date to visit everyone at the old house and up until 1994, she was still alive and well into her eighties.

The nearby Slades boat yard was now up for sale, so Daphne and Tommy bought it for Tommy to go into boat design after the war.

The old white cabin boat, which was used for their honeymoon in 1932, was now retired and suitably placed on the lawn in their garden at Menabilly for the children to play in.

In the meantime, Tommy bought a CFV vessel he'd seen in Singapore and had it brought back to England on a troop ship to be refitted in Hunkin's boat yard over at Bodinnick-by-Fowey, and named it *Fanny Rosa*.

# Chapter 30

## *Sir Tommy and Lady Browning*

Daphne continued to write and type quietly in the wooden hut in her garden at Menabilly, heated by an oil heater, whilst Tommy, was away in the Far East. He then retired from the Army and was knighted in the 1946 Honours List (making Daphne Lady Browning), and eventually joined the Royal Household.

During the winter of 1946 Cornwall experienced one of the hardest winters on record — when the heavy snow fell and froze like Siberia, freezing the household pipes for weeks. It became so cold people even slept with their clothes on. Electricity was off for days in places making it necessary to use candles and oil lamps once again. The old house of Menabilly was snowed in completely.

# Chapter 31

## *New York*

By the autumn of 1947 Daphne had an occasion to go to New York, taking Flavia, Kits and governess Tod with her; Tessa having gone away to boarding school.

They all took the Cornish Riviera express train from Par station to Paddington, where they were met by Tommy, who afterwards saw them off by train again, en route to Southampton, where they embarked on the *Queen Mary*, which at that time was like a floating hotel. On board also was a famous passenger, the actress Greta Garbo!

Daphne was in New York to attend a court case against her, because it was said at that time that she had copied her book *Rebecca* from a book by someone else, called *Blind Windows*, but in fact it bore no resemblance to *Rebecca* at all.

Whilst in New York, amongst her dinner guests she met Noel Coward. Daphne was forty, and by the December 1947 the court case had ended. She had won the day, but it had worn her out with nervous exhaustion.

Travelling back again on the *Queen Mary* and dreading the cold wintry conditions at Menabilly, the family were met at Southampton where they boarded the boat train for London. Daphne collapsed into bed and was treated by a visiting doctor who ordered quietness and rest. She remained unwell almost until Christmas, but once home again at her beloved old house, she soon felt well again to decorate it in time for Christmas 1947.

## Chapter 32

# *A Busy Life*

The mine disposal group going around after the war cleared all the landmines from the Cornish Pridmouth Bay area, which made it safe again for the du Maurier/Browning family to resume their swimming and picnics. Tessa was still away at boarding school at Rousham near Granny Browning. This pleased her very much.

No secret was ever made of the fact that socialising was never Daphne's scene. Whilst in London and sharing a flat Tommy enjoyed his dinner engagements with the famous, such as the actor Douglas Fairbanks Jnr., and being a lover of the ballet, became friendly with Margot Fonteyn.

The year of 1949 saw Daphne's latest book *The Parasites* completed and her play *September Tide* was put on in the West End with Gertrude Lawrence in the lead. Gertie was introduced to her by Noel Coward when she was in New York in 1947 attending the court case, and had her in mind for this play which also starred Michael Gough and a young boy called Bryan Forbes!

Tommy loved archery and taught Daphne and Kits, as well as Margot Fonteyn, Tom's ballet friend. She was invited down to Menabilly to stay one weekend and to learn archery for her ballet part in *Silvier*. Margot arrived in Cornwall on the night train. For this special famous friend breakfast was arranged on the lawn, laid up with a tablecloth, cut glass tumblers and silver coffee pot. Tommy became an expert on ballet and always watched Margot perform when in London.

Menabilly always looked particularly at its best during May. Years earlier part of the garden had been used as a nursery for Kew Gardens.

## Chapter 33

## *Alone*

As Daphne liked eating alone, the children were never allowed to eat with grown-ups until they were at least twelve years of age. She spent her time at Menabilly in her wooden hut with her typewriter. Here, she worked six days a week, part-time; her books now taking between four to six months to complete. Each book totally drained her of energy. With the children away at boarding school, Daphne spent her time writing and walking, and in the evenings in the long room at Menabilly, surrounded by her Chippendale furniture. Although she spent little on clothes, Daphne was still attractive.

Tommy's job after his retirement from the Army, being involved in the royal household of Princess Elizabeth and Prince Philip, meant he accompanied the royal couple on foreign trips to Canada, Australia and other Commonwealth countries.

Daphne's book *My Cousin Rachel* was published in 1951. It was so named after Rachel Carew-Pole of Antony House, Saltash. This was also made into a film and produced in Hollywood, starring Richard Burton and Olivia de Havilland.

## Chapter 34

## *Tommy's Royal Duties*

In 1952, whilst on a foreign visit to Kenya, Princess Elizabeth received the sad news of the death of her beloved father King George VI, so Tommy accompanied the royal couple back to England where the Princess became Queen Elizabeth II.

Tommy was appointed treasurer to the Duke of Edinburgh and, in February 1953, both Tommy and Daphne were honoured guests at the Queen's coronation ceremony in London.

With Daphne remaining in Cornwall, Tommy commuted at weekends.

Although Tessa and Flavia didn't get on too well until reaching their teens, they eventually became the best of friends. Flavia went on to study Art in Paris and also took an acting course, eventually painting as a hobby, she designed book jackets for her mother's books.

# Chapter 35

## *Family Weddings*

A family wedding — 3rd March 1954. Tessa married at twenty-one to Captain Peter de Zulueta of the Welsh Guards, at St James' church, London with sister Flavia as bridesmaid. A reception of several hundred guests was held at The Savoy, where Tommy was a director. For the honeymoon the couple flew off to Switzerland, returning to live in a house at Ascot.

In October 1955 Daphne went to France. Her latest book, *The Scapegoat* had taken six months to write. This was also made into a film starring Alec Guinness and Bette Davis. Tessa had a daughter called Marie-Therése; the Brownings' first grandchild.

On the 17th June 1956 there was another grand family wedding — Flavia, at nineteen married Captain Alastair Tower, officer of the Coldstream Guards, at St Peter's church, Eaton Square.

Sadly on the 28th November 1957 Daphne's mother Muriel died, twenty-three years after her father Gerald. With her health failing since the end of the war, Muriel and a nurse had moved into Ferryside, to spend the last seven years of her life with her daughter, Angela. (Her third daughter Jeanne was living almost permanently abroad.)

1959, in London, a son named Rupert was born to Flavia, and also a son called Paul to Tessa.

# Chapter 36

## *Alone at Menabilly with Tommy*

With Tessa and Flavia now both married and living away from Cornwall, Daphne lived alone at Menabilly without any of her family. Her son Kits, now eighteen years of age, pursued a career in films and became a personal assistant to Daphne's old friend, the director Sir Carol Reed.

In April 1959 her friend Foy Quiller-Couch asked her to complete her father's unfinished manuscript of his last novel, *Castle Dor*. This she did, and it was later published in 1962.

Tommy was becoming very tired and unwell, so retired from royal service at the age of sixty-two. He spent the summer of 1959 at Menabilly with Daphne, gradually recuperating but experiencing constant nausea due to a liver problem.

For the next six years (until his death in 1965), Tommy and Daphne enjoyed a very friendly and affectionate companionship.

By October 1959, Tommy's health had improved to enable him and Daphne to live busy lives. He became the first group controller of civil defence in Cornwall and soon became deputy lieutenant of Cornwall as well.

# Chapter 37

## *Sad Times*

1960 was a sad year. First, the death of Daphne's cousin and special friend Peter Davies, who committed suicide by throwing himself under a subway train. Secondly, the death of Dr Rashleigh, who so long ago inherited Menabilly but let it fall into disrepair until he allowed Daphne to lease the old house from him back in 1943.

Again, Daphne knew she could never own Menabilly. For the past seventeen years it had been a constant worry to her that the Rashleigh family might want the house back again one day, but as long as Dr Rashleigh was alive, she knew she was safe in her beloved house. He didn't want to live there, but now he was dead the house and estate were passed on to his nephew Phillip Rashleigh, which opened up a serious possibility that he might feel differently about the family house, and therefore may want to live in it himself. But Daphne always hoped and prayed this would never happen.

## Chapter 38

## *Royal Guests*

April 1962, with the publication of *Castle Dor*, it was also an Indian summer for Daphne and Tommy! She was fifty-five, young-looking and slender; he was sixty-six, and royal guests were due to arrive at Menabilly!

Daphne and Tommy entertained Her Majesty the Queen and Prince Philip to a family tea whilst they were visiting the West Country. Her Majesty complimented them on their lovely old country house.

During this time Tommy's health began to give cause for concern.

E

## Chapter 39

## *The End in Sight*

By March 1963 Daphne was able to visit Rome with Flavia, but between March '63 and 1965 (with the death of Dr Rashleigh), Daphne's world turned upside down, with the strong possibility of having to leave Menabilly — the rambling, old family home that her children had grown up in and loved. This worry had been in her mind since the signing of the lease in 1943.

Her life continued, writing and walking in the woods with her dogs, sometimes with Tommy, lunch with very selective friends and watching her TV — but never discussing leaving Menabilly, which she had so lovingly restored after years of decay. Only favoured visitors would ever be shown around the house and grounds.

When she finally came to terms with having to leave this house, which had been as much a lover to her as any man could ever be — inwardly she was deeply angry, although outwardly she remained friendly towards the Rashleigh family, but never forgave them.

Tommy was fond of Menabilly, but when the worst happened and the new heir Phillip Rashleigh made it clear that he was not going to extend their lease (which was due to expire in 1968) as he wanted to return and live in it himself, Tommy did his best to reconcile

Daphne to the inevitable.

Phillip Rashleigh never understood why his uncle Dr Rashleigh had not wanted to live in that house — but Daphne always knew she could never own it because it was always quite likely that one day the Rashleigh family would return to live in it again.

The press interviewed Daphne regarding this matter, who told them how she felt at being made to leave Menabilly after over twenty years in residence. Phillip Rashleigh was not very popular, but did offer Daphne and Tommy a very acceptable alternative, the Rashleigh's dower house called Kilmarth, about half a mile away from Menabilly, overlooking Par Bay. This was also an old house, used in the past by a Professor Charles Singer.

It was still always a mystery why Daphne and Tommy, with all their wealth, didn't ever buy themselves a beautiful property in Cornwall to avoid the sad situation they now found themselves in and which was causing so much anxiety. Daphne had more than enough money to buy any Cornish house on an estate of any size or age that she may choose, especially at the low house prices in the 1960s.

# Chapter 40

## *Kilmarth*

In May 1964 Tommy launched a new boat in Fowey called the *Ygdrasil III* — a boat of his own design, and son Kits married Olive.

During this year Tommy encouraged Daphne to look and think positive about the move from Menabilly to Kilmarth, for which they visited the nearby house together many times to look it over and discuss the improvements required, etc., as it had also been neglected for many years and was in need of repair.

Although Kilmarth was not as old as Menabilly, it was quite big enough for two, plus their visiting children and grandchildren. Tommy remarked at the time that he could see themselves there in due course!

So once again they duly engaged an architect, obtained builders' estimates, etc., for the restoration of Kilmarth, and it was agreed that Phillip Rashleigh was not going to move into Menabilly in a hurry.

# Chapter 41

## *Tommy's Farewell*

By Christmas 1964, at the age of sixty-eight years, Tommy was admitted to St Mary's Hospital, Paddington, "under observation" which resulted in major surgery in January 1965.

By the end of January 1965 Tommy returned to Menabilly to convalesce, and a few weeks later he signed the lease for Kilmarth (although Daphne would remain at Menabilly for another four years, until 1969, when she officially moved into Kilmarth).

Within weeks of signing this new lease Tommy became so ill he needed full-time nursing — day and night — so that he could remain at home at Menabilly until he sadly collapsed and died on the 14th March 1965.

Married to Daphne for thirty-three years, only his children and family attended the cremation, after which his ashes were scattered near her writing hut on the Menabilly estate.

For the last few years Daphne and Tommy had shared both companionship and affection, but with Tommy's death, the move to Kilmarth was now on the horizon.

## Chapter 42

## *Alone — Without Tommy*

With the loss of Tommy, Daphne's move to Kilmarth was delayed and it was agreed that she could stay on at Menabilly until the summer of 1969 whilst Kilmarth was made habitable for her and the various improvements were completed, as per all the plans before Tommy's death,

In 1967 Daphne's picture book *Vanishing Cornwall,* compiled with her son Kits who was now a photographer, was published. He was married to Olive, an Irish girl, with two young sons, Frederick and Robert (Edward and Grace arrived in the early 1970s).

Their boat yard was now sold and Daphne spent her time going to Kilmarth to oversee the work being carried out over there before her eventual move in 1969.

In the meantime she commenced her latest novel *The House on the Strand* which was inspired and written around Kilmarth, with Daphne continuing to wear her usual attire of slacks, jersey and anorak, accompanied by her dogs. Two years later it was published.

Her wealth continued to grow — much going into family trusts to avoid tax.

Summer 1969 — and the move to Kilmarth!

# Chapter 43

## *The Move*

After twenty-six happy years at Menabilly, the day arrived at last to move to the nearby newly-renovated old dower house, with a slated front but 20th Century additions to each side of it. Gradually Daphne grew to accept her new abode.

The removal vans arrived to move her furniture and contents of packed cases, piled in the forty-five-foot "long room" at Menabilly. Even Tommy's old white honeymoon boat the *Ygdrasil* was moved from the Menabilly lawn to the grounds at Kilmarth, where Daphne had the overgrown gardens cleared, and put in order.

At Kilmarth there was much wildlife, such as badgers, foxes, owls, jackdaws, swallows, and butterflies, plus a shed facing out across Carlyon Bay. A steep path led from Kilmarth across a field to a beach and at sixty-two years of age Daphne was still active, fit and mentally very lively.

## Chapter 44

# *Dame Daphne*

In the Queen's Birthday's Honours List for that summer of 1969 Daphne was made DBE, to become Dame Daphne du Maurier, and was therefore invited to Buckingham Palace on the 23rd July 1969 for the presentation, after which she had to face life without her beloved Menabilly and Tommy.

Two main events in her life always remained in her thoughts, 'til the day she died; her first sight of Menabilly in 1928, and how Tommy had sailed into her life in his white boat that summer of 1932.

Her great friendship with the Cornish historian and writer Dr A. L. Rowse continued, both of them living in large isolated old Cornish houses and both with housekeepers. He lived at Trenarren and she at Kilmarth, where she regularly entertained him to lunch, with the help of Esther to cook for them — no wine, only water was consumed!

Dame Daphne's new house was now in order with all her family belongings and furniture around her, where she created a new long room, a TV room and a dining room, so that when all the doors were left open she could see from one end of the house to the other, which gave her a great feeling of space, with French windows leading out into the gardens where Tommy's old honeymoon boat (now painted grey, for the grandchildren to play in) was laid-up on the lawn, retired!

# Chapter 45

## *The Last Novel*

In 1970 Tessa's marriage to Major Peter de Zulueta ended, but she went on to marry again, to David, the son of Field Marshal Montgomery (which would have pleased her father without doubt).

The film *Don't Look Now* taken from one of Daphne's short stories was released in 1971, starring Donald Sutherland and Julie Christie. She had thought of the story some years previously when she visited Venice with her sister.

Whilst she continued the long daily walks with her dogs (weather permitting), she spent her evenings eating her supper in front of the television, becoming quite a TV addict which kept her up to date on the national and international news as she grew older — she also enjoyed the 'soaps' at that time!

During the early 1970s at Kilmarth, after *Rule Britannia* was finished, Daphne wrote two nonfiction books about The Bacon brothers, Antony and Francis Bacon. Much research went into the writing of these books, resulting in, Vol. I, *Golden Lads* — published in 1975 and Vol. II, *The Winding Stair* — published in 1976.

Daphne found working on the Bacon books absorbing and very enjoyable, having to search through archive material and being chauffeured around by her son Kits, then back home again to Kilmarth to write about it.

# Chapter 46

## *Life at Kilmarth*

Flavia was now divorced from Major Alastair Tower. The marriage had resulted in one son, called Rupert. Daphne at Kilmarth was seldom out of corduroy trousers, anoraks and sea boots — similar to those as worn by her over the years.

Only a handful of books remained now to be written, including an autobiography of her early years called *Growing Pains* which was published in 1977. She always kept diaries from her teenage years up until her marriage in 1932, when her diaries ceased.

There were also a collection of essays which were written years earlier, together with some short stories, plus an essay on her house move from Menabilly to Kilmarth.

Daphne's mornings were spent researching and writing, and in the afternoons (weather permitting) out walking her dogs. Her small suppers eaten on her lap in the evenings in the room which was full of family past and present; Gerald's photos, portraits, canes, sticks and various swordsticks. Then to bed, to say nightly prayers before sleeping.

On Sundays Daphne preferred to be alone — no visits or visitations, and after lunch/coffee, she would set off again for her usual walk.

Although often referred to as a recluse, she didn't see herself as such; her family visiting her regularly and she visiting them. It's just that she liked her own company!

After *Growing Pains* she eventually became more reclusive, and for the next decade (1979-1989), would walk the woods and grounds of her beloved Menabilly.

The new resident member of the Rashleigh family who now lived there must have been aware of her visitations. She would set off across the grounds at Kilmarth for her cross-country walk only to find herself drawn to the Menabilly estate to watch all the work that was going on there to clear all the overgrown gardens, and the cutting back of the shrubs, etc. (Also in 1980, to watch the demolition of that unsafe Victorian wing attached to Menabilly, together with the gate house which was also considered unsafe at that time.)

Ten years after Daphne's move to Kilmarth, in 1979, she learned that a member of the Rashleigh family was unwell, so called at Menabilly to enquire how they were and taking with her some apples from her orchard. Whereupon she was invited in and after that was a regular visitor to Menabilly, going over for tea at least once a week, and on Daphne's birthday, 13th May, Veronica Rashleigh would give her a bunch of lilac from her favourite tree at Menabilly!

# Chapter 47

## *The Last Decade*

Throughout Daphne's latter years (in the 1980s), she and her sister Angela (health permitting) would weekly visit each other at Kilmarth and Ferryside, and at the same time kept in touch by telephone, ringing each other every day at 9 a.m. Their sister Jeanne lived in a thatched house in Devon with a friend, but would write to each other regularly. They were a united family, as were the previous du Maurier generation.

The film *A Bridge Too Far* was released at the cinemas, with Dirk Bogarde cast in the film part of Tommy, in this true story about The Battle of Arnhem and the Normandy landings.

Daphne, no longer going to London, refused to see this war film, as she felt that no actor, however good, could adequately portray her late husband Tommy Browning. The film was substantially different from the book which she had enjoyed.

Her wealth continued to grow due to the royalties from the twenty-five books she had written, and made her one of the richest writers.

For over ten years she tried her best to fight off depression. Writing her books for all those years and using her imagination had been *everything* to her.

Kits and Tessa visited her often. Flavia had remarried in 1981 to Sir Peter Leng and was living in the West Country with their cats and dogs, and enjoying their garden.

1982 and a crisis! Daphne's doctor and housekeeper, Esther Rowe, noticed what at first appeared to be Daphne suffering from a severe nervous breakdown, but it later appeared to be more than that. Was it the start of Alzheimer's disease or a slight stroke, which left her mentally confused?

Dr A. L. Rowse, her old family friend, remarked that after that everything folded up — she wouldn't visit friends or allow them to visit her — just her family.

The last few years were deeply unhappy ones. She still walked within the grounds of Kilmarth with her dogs but only rarely went further afield — either to Menabilly or Ferryside.

As time passed by Daphne became increasingly confused, and her publishers formally announced there would be no more du Maurier books.

Eventually Daphne became so confused and frail, that a nurse was engaged to live-in and help Esther to look after her. For a few months before her death she seemed quite unaware of what was going on around her, and towards the end of her life found visits from the local vicar Canon Oatey most comforting, although in life Daphne had no religious certainty — not like her sisters — Angela who was High Anglican and Jeanne, a Roman Catholic — but in the basement of Kilmarth Daphne had her own little chapel, and became quite religious in her last couple of years.

On the morning of 19th April 1989 Esther went in to wake Daphne as usual, to find she had sadly died peacefully in her sleep at Kilmarth, where she had been a widow, on her own for twenty-four years.

Many tributes poured in from all over the world from the many fans who had never met her, but were her devoted readers all through the years.

At her own request Daphne was cremated and a memorial service was held in her memory at Tregaminion church on the Menabilly estate, attended by only her family. The date and time were not publicised for obvious reasons, and her ashes were scattered on the land she so loved, at Kilmarth by her family and mourned by her devoted housekeeper who had supported and cared for her for over thirty years.

Her son Kits was executor of her estate, and in her Will Daphne left approximately a quarter of a million pounds.

After Daphne's death, the book *Enchanted Cornwall,* which was a compilation of Daphne's writings and recordings over her life time, with special emphasis on Cornwall, was published. It is now in paperback and called *Daphne du Maurier's Cornwall — A Memoir.*

In September 1989, sorting through Daphne's estate, certain items from Kilmarth were auctioned, including her William IV writing desk and mahogany Sheraton writing table, on which (it was thought) Daphne had written both *Jamaica Inn* and *Rebecca.*

Because of her frugality at Kilmarth, most of the objects were badly damaged, worn or badly affected by dampness. Flat surfaces were marked with rings made from hot tea/coffee cups, but this did not deter the loyal fans who descended in their masses on the day of the auction. The prices for Daphne memorabilia proved staggering.

Her Sheraton writing table was bought by the owners of The Jamaica Inn, Bolventor, Bodmin, where it is now on show in their du Maurier Museum.

On that day devoted fans were so happy to buy anything connected with their reclusive idol, who until the end maintained her ritual of walking alone, keeping herself to herself — she just liked being alone!